TABLE OF CONTENTS

This record embodies a new technique being used by Music Minus One. We have recorded the ensemble in two-track stereo. This enables the buyer to lower the right channel of his stereo player, removing the solo part. He can then play along with the ensemble, which will be heard on the left speaker. Conversely, lowering the left hand speaker will remove the ensemble, leaving the solo part in bold relief for study and emulation.

INTRODUCTION

The recorder is one of the oldest woodwind instruments, and produces a beautiful, soft sound when it is played correctly. There are different sizes of recorders, but the one you are playing is called the soprano.

Learning to play your recorder can be a lot of fun. We have included many songs that you know, and if you follow the directions in this book and listen carefully to the record, you will understand more about your recorder and the language of music. Good luck!

THE AUTHORS

MUSICAL TERMS AND SYMBOLS

You should know a few musical terms and symbols before you begin:

Music is written on a <u>staff</u>. This staff has 5 lines and 4 spaces. These lines and spaces are counted from the bottom.

We get different pitches or tones by placing <u>notes</u> on the lines and in the spaces.

The <u>Treble Clef or G Clef</u> shows that the second line of the staff is called G. The clef circles the second line. All the songs in this book are written in the Treble Clef.

Vertical lines on the staff are called <u>bar lines</u>. The space between the bar lines is called a <u>measure</u>. <u>A double bar line</u> shows that you have come to the end of a section or piece of music.

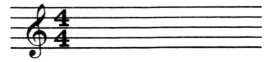

MEASURE   MEASURE

In the <u>time signature</u> the top number shows how many counts there are in one measure. The bottom number shows what kind of note gets one count.

MMO 220

mmo

Music Minus One

MMO CD 3338
MMO Cass. 220

LET'S PLAY THE RECORDER:
A METHOD FOR CHILDREN

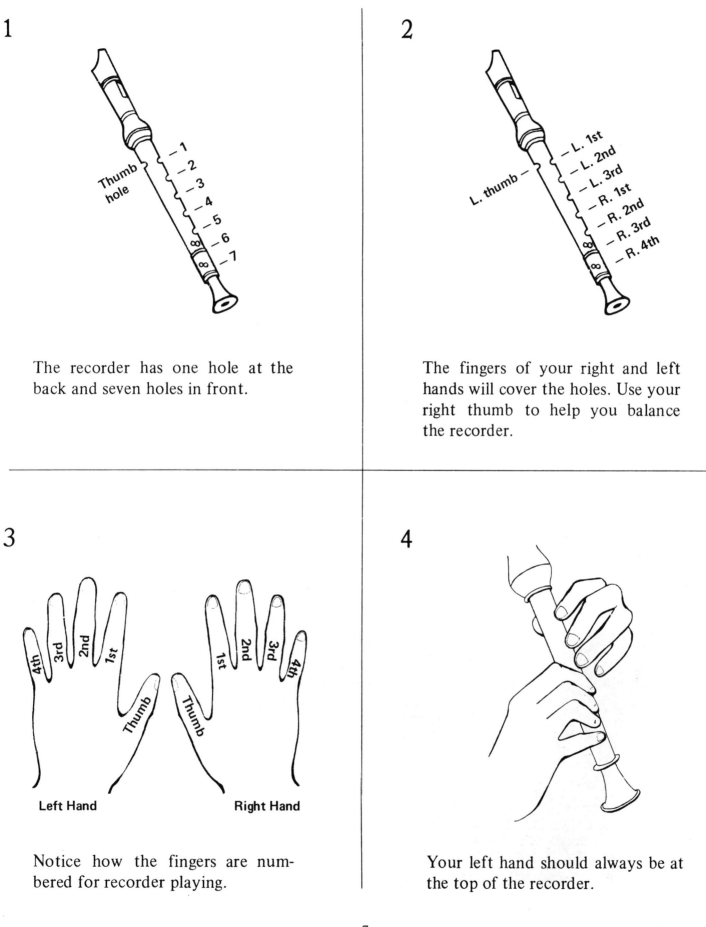

1

The recorder has one hole at the back and seven holes in front.

2

The fingers of your right and left hands will cover the holes. Use your right thumb to help you balance the recorder.

3

Notice how the fingers are numbered for recorder playing.

4

Your left hand should always be at the top of the recorder.

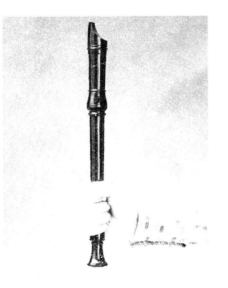

STEP 1

Hold your recorder with your right hand near the bottom holes.

STEP 2

Cover the thumb-hole with your left thumb.

STEP 3

Cover the first hole with your left first finger. Keep your left thumb on the thumb hole.

STEP 4

Open your right hand and balance the recorder on your right thumb between the fourth and fifth holes.

STEP 5

Place the recorder on your lower lip and in front of your teeth. Close your mouth gently around the recorder.

STEP 6

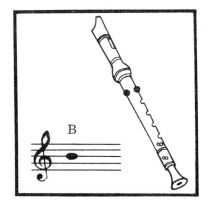

Make a silent "daah" sound (this is called tonguing), and gently blow into your recorder. The note you are playing is called "B". Practice it a few times before turning the page.

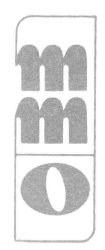

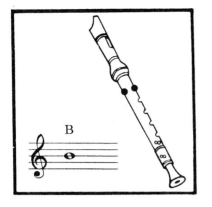

In $\frac{4}{4}$ time there are four counts in each measure. A <u>quarter note</u> (♩) gets one count and a quarter rest (𝄽) gets one count of silence. A <u>breath mark</u> (') tells you when to take a breath in the music.

SIDE A - BAND 1

1. THIRD LINE "B"

4 taps (1 measure) precede music.

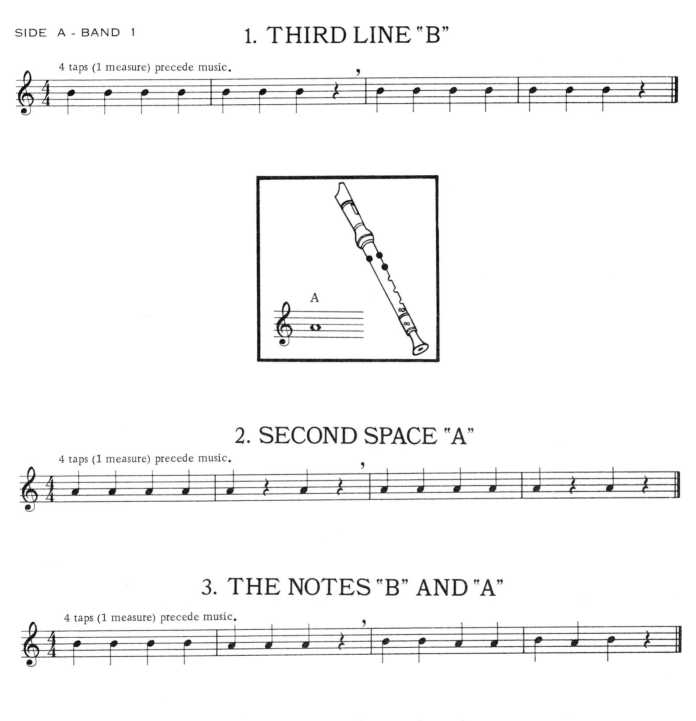

2. SECOND SPACE "A"

4 taps (1 measure) precede music.

3. THE NOTES "B" AND "A"

4 taps (1 measure) precede music.

Breathe through your mouth, not through your nose.

A <u>half note</u> (♩) gets two counts. A <u>half rest</u> (▬) gets two counts of silence.

4. PIERROT   (Excerpt)

French

SIDE A - BAND 2

5. MARY HAD A LITTLE LAMB

Traditional

6. SUO GÂN

Welsh

Remember to blow gently and tongue gently. (Think of "daah")

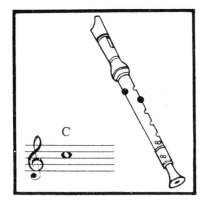

In $\frac{2}{4}$ time there are two counts in each measure.

7. A PARIS

French

4 taps (2 measures) precede music.

8. JUBA

American

4 taps (2 measures) precede music.

9. CAPUCINE

French

4 taps (2 measures) precede music.

A <u>whole note</u> (○) gets four counts.
A <u>whole rest</u> (▬) gets four counts
of silence.

10. LIGHTLY ROW   (Duet)

German

A duet is a piece for two players. Learn both parts.   4 taps (1 measure) precede music.

11. GO TELL AUNT RHODIE

American

4 taps (1 measure) precede music.

When you play the note D be sure that your right thumb stays
under the recorder.

In $\frac{3}{4}$ time there are three counts in each measure. A quarter note (♩) gets one count, a half note (♪) gets two counts, and a dotted half note (♩.) gets three counts.

12. LITTLE BIRD

French

SIDE A - BAND 4

13. CUCKOO

German

14. FAIS DO-DO

French

15. WINTER, FAREWELL

German

6 taps (2 measures) precede music.

16. OATS, PEAS, BEANS AND BARLEY GROW

American

6 taps (2 measures) precede music.

SIDE A - BAND 5

17. IN MAY

German

6 taps (2 measures) precede music.

Congratulations! You have learned a lot about music. You know five notes, four note values and rests, and three time signatures. You will be finding out more about music in this book, but always remember to review the songs you have already learned.

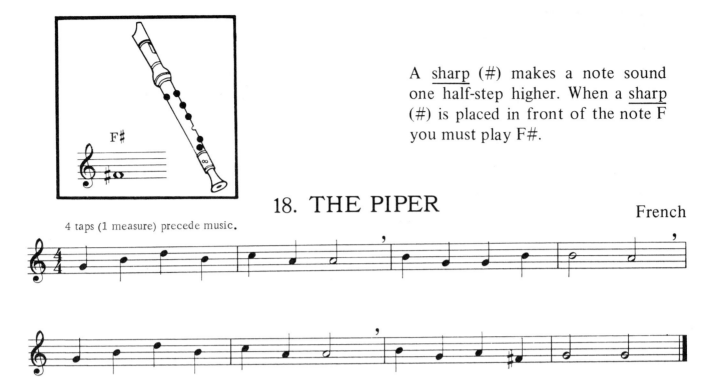

A sharp (#) makes a note sound one half-step higher. When a sharp (#) is placed in front of the note F you must play F#.

18. THE PIPER

French

4 taps (1 measure) precede music.

When a sharp (#) is placed on the fifth line of the staff, between the clef sign and the time signature it becomes a key signature. This tells you to play every F in the piece as F#.

19. LULLABY

Polish

6 taps (2 measures) precede music.

20. DANCE

V. Hausmann, 1600-

4 taps (1 measure) precede music.

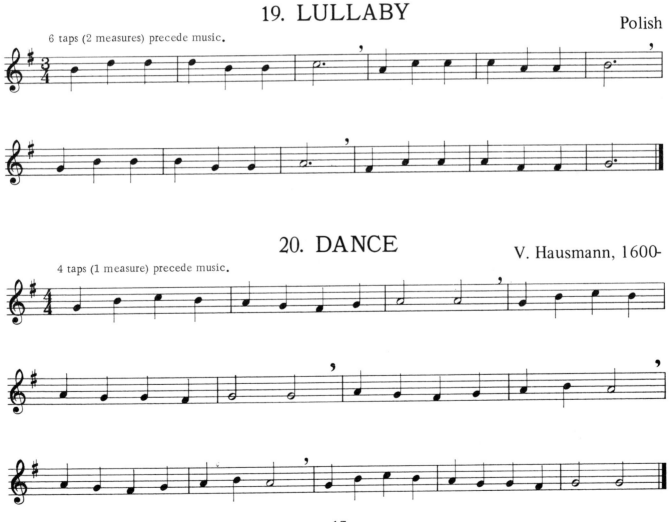

A repeat sign 𝄇 tells you to go back to the beginning and play the music again.

21. TEMPLE BELLS

Chinese

4 taps (1 measure) precede music.

C is the same as $\frac{4}{4}$ time. There are four counts in each measure.

22. WARRIORS BRAVE

Indian

4 taps (1 measure) precede music.

23. THE DOVE

Welsh

6 taps (2 measures) precede music.

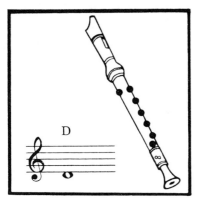

A <u>staccato mark</u> ( ) tells you to play the notes short and separated from each other.

24. GOOD KING WENCESLAS

Christmas Carol

4 taps (1 measure) precede music.

25. HOP, HOP, HOP

German

4 taps (1 measure) precede music.

26. THE BEE

German

4 taps (1 measure) precede music.

Listen to the record. Do you hear how gently the staccato notes are played?

Two eighth notes (♪♪) equal one quarter note. They get one count. Each count has a downbeat and an upbeat. If you tap your foot, the first eighth note is on the downbeat and the second eighth note on the upbeat. Or think 1 "and" (♪♪).

1 &

27. OZARK MOUNTAIN MELODY

American

4 taps (2 measures) precede music.

1 2 & 1 2 & 1 2 1 2

SIDE B - BAND 2

28. JINGLE BELLS (Duet)

Christmas Song

4 taps (1 measure) precede music.

Player No. 1

Player No. 2

No. 1

No. 2

No. 1

No. 2

No. 1

No. 2

MMO 220

Some pieces do not begin on the first count of the measure. When this happens it is called an <u>incomplete measure</u>. The notes that are needed to complete the measure are found in the last measure of the piece.

29. WE WISH YOU A MERRY CHRISTMAS

5 taps (1 and 2/3 measures) precede music.

Christmas Carol

<u>D.C. al Fine</u>-Da Capo or D.C. means to go back to the beginning of the piece, and play to the measure marked <u>Fine</u>.

30. THE BRIDGE OF AVIGNON

French

4 taps (2 measures) precede music.

31. THANKS

Danish

4 taps (1 measure) precede music.

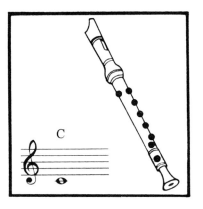

C

32. LIZA JANE

American

4 taps (1 measure) precede music.

33. TIDEO

American

4 taps (1 measure) precede music.

When you play the low "C", be sure to cover all the holes completely, and blow very gently.

F

These <u>repeat signs</u> (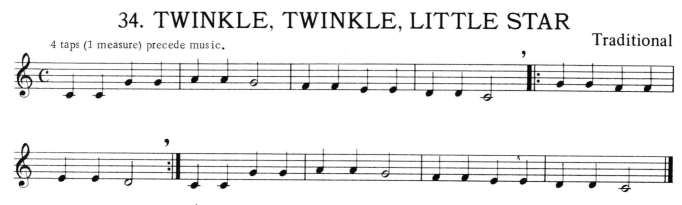) tell you to repeat the music that is between the double dotted bar lines.

34. TWINKLE, TWINKLE, LITTLE STAR

Traditional

4 taps (1 measure) precede music.

An <u>eighth note</u> (♪) is one-half as long as a quarter note and gets one-half of a count. An <u>eighth rest</u> (ʔ) gets one-half of a count of silence.

35. HANUKKAH

Hebrew

4 taps (2 measures) precede music.

36. THIS OLD MAN

Children's Song

4 taps (1 measure) precede music.

A <u>tie</u> (♩ ♩) connects two notes of the same pitch. The second note is held and counted but not played.

37. HOLLA HI, HOLLA HO

Bavarian

4 taps (2 measures) precede music.

38. BLOW THE MAN DOWN

Sea Chantey

5 taps (1 and 2/3 measures) precede music.

A <u>flat</u> (♭) makes a note sound one half-step lower. When a <u>flat</u> (♭) is placed on the third line of the staff, between the clef sign and the time signature it becomes a <u>key signature</u>. This tells you to play every B in the piece as B♭.

39. FRÈRE JACQUES

French

4 taps (1 measure) precede music.

SIDE B - BAND 5

40. DAISY BELL

American

6 taps (2 measures) precede music.

A dot placed after a note gets one-half the value of the note. A <u>dotted</u> <u>quarter note</u> and an <u>eighth note</u> together (♩.   ♪) get two counts.

1 & 2 &

41. AURA LEE

American

4 taps (1 measure) precede music.

A <u>fermata sign</u> (⌢) placed above a note tells you to hold that note a little longer than its usual count.

42. AULD LANG SYNE

Scotch

7 taps (1 and 3/4 measures) precede music.

43. AMERICA

English

6 taps (2 measures) precede music.

44. HYMN TO JOY

Ludwig van Beethoven, 1770-1827

4 taps (1 measure) precede music.

The first and second ending signs  tell you to play the first ending and repeat the section. Then skip the first ending and go directly to the second ending.

45. THE MARINES' HYMN

American

3 taps (1 and 1/2 measures) precede music.

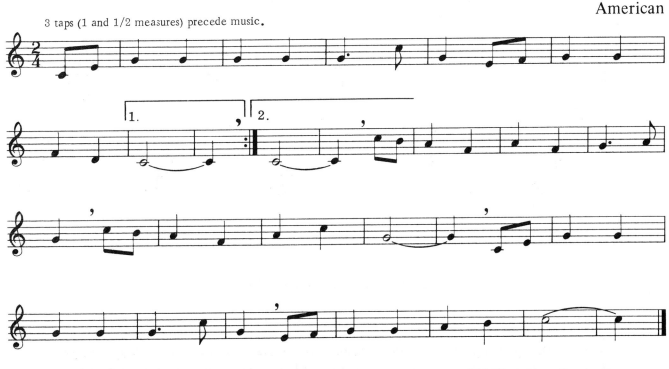

WE HOPE YOU'VE ENJOYED FINDING OUT ABOUT MUSIC AND YOUR RECORDER, AND THAT YOU WILL CONTINUE TO EXPLORE THE GREAT AMOUNT OF MUSIC WRITTEN FOR THIS LOVELY INSTRUMENT.

FINGERING CHART FOR SOPRANO RECORDER
English (Baroque) Fingering

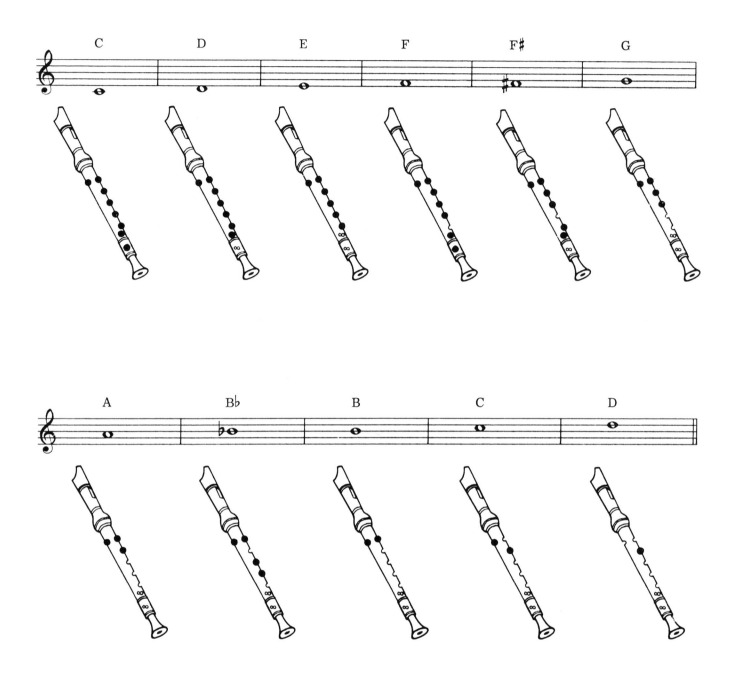

O = open hole; ● = closed hole.

The recorder in this Kit has the English fingering system. This is traditionally the only true recorder fingering system. However, there are some recorders that have the German system, but they are inferior in pitch and should be avoided. The German fingering system needs a different fingering for F and F#.

INDEX OF SONGS

Illustrations and Fingering Diagrams by Justine Schachter
Photographs by Ken Haas

Music Minus One TROMBONE Compact Discs

___	MMO CD	3901	Easy Solos, Student Series, Beginning Level
___	MMO CD	3902	Easy Solos, Student Series. Beg/Intermediate Level
___	MMO CD	3903	Easy Jazz Duets, 1 -3 rd Student Level
___	MMO CD	3904	Baroque, Brass & Beyond - Brass Quintet Music
___	MMO CD	3905	Music For B rass Ensemble

Choice selections for the Trombone, drawn from the very best solo literature for the instrument. The pieces are performed by the foremost virtuosi of our time, artists affiliated with the New York Philharmonic, Boston, Chicago, Cleveland and Philadelphia Orchestras. The Julliard School, Curtis Institute of Music, Indiana University, University of Toronto and Metropolitan Opera Orchestra.

___	MMO CD	3911	Beginning Contest Solos
___	MMO CD	3912	Beginning Contest Solos
___	MMO CD	3913	Keith Brown, Professor, Indiana University - Intermediate
___	MMO CD	3914	Jay Friedman, Chicago Symphony - Intermediate
___	MMO CD	3915	Keith Brown, Professor, Indiana University - Advanced
___	MMO CD	3916	Per Brevig, Metropolitan Opera - Advanced
___	MMO CD	3917	Keith Brown, Professor, Indiana University - Advanced
___	MMO CD	3918	Jay Friedman, Chicago Symphony - Advanced
___	MMO CD	3919	Per Brevig, Metropolitan Opera - Advanced

Music Minus One VOCALIST Compact Discs

___	MMO CD	4001	Schubert German Lieder for High Voice
___	MMO CD	4002	Schubert German Lieder for Low Voice
___	MMO CD	4003	Schubert German Lieder, Vol. 2, for High Voice
___	MMO CD	4004	Schubert German Lieder, Vol. 2, for Low Voice
___	MMO CD	4005	Brahms German Lieder for High Voice
___	MMO CD	4006	Brahms German Lieder for Low Voice
___	MMO CD	4007	Everybody's Favorite Songs for High Voice
___	MMO CD	4008	Everybody's Favorite Songs for Low Voice
___	MMO CD	4009	Everybody's Favorite Songs, Vol. 2, High Voice
___	MMO CD	4010	Everybody's Favorite Songs, Vol. 2 Low Voice
___	MMO CD	4011	17th/18th Century Italian songs High Voice
___	MMO CD	4012	17th/18th Century Italian songs Low Voice
___	MMO CD	4013	17th/18th Century Italian songs #2 High Voice
___	MMO CD	4014	17th/18th Century Italian songs #2 Low Voice
___	MMO CD	4015	Famous Soprano Arias
___	MMO CD	4016	Famous Mezzo-Soprano Arias
___	MMO CD	4017	Famous Tenor Arias
___	MMO CD	4018	Famous Baritone Arias
___	MMO CD	4019	Famous Bass Arias
___	MMO CD	4020	Wolf German Lieder For High Voice
___	MMO CD	4021	Wolf German Lieder For Low Voice
___	MMO CD	4022	Strauss German Lieder For High Voice
___	MMO CD	4023	Strauss German Lieder For Low Voice
___	MMO CD	4024	Schumann German Lieder for High Voice
___	MMO CD	4025	Schumann German Lieder for Low Voice
___	MMO CD	4026	Mozart Arias for Soprano
___	MMO CD	4027	Verdi Arias for Soprano
___	MMO CD	4028	Italian Arias For Soprano
___	MMO CD	4029	French Arias For Soprano
___	MMO CD	4030	Soprano Oratorio Arias
___	MMO CD	4031	Alto Oratorio Arias
___	MMO CD	4032	Tenor Oratorio Arias
___	MMO CD	4033	Bass Oratorio Arias

In a field which is dominated by the vocal soloist, John Wustman is one of the few accompanists in this country who has achieved renown and critical acclaim in this most challenging of art forms. Mr. Wustman has developed that rare quality of bringing a strength and character to his accompaniments which create a true collaboration between the singer and the pianist. And this is as it should be, for in the art song especially, the piano part is not a mere rhythmic and tonal background, but an integral part of the c composer's intent and creation. Thus, on these records, Mr. Wustman provides not only the necessary accompaniment but also through his artistry a stylistic and interpretive suggestion for the study of music. Among the many artists he has accompanied in the past years are: Gianna d'Angelo, Irina Arkhipova, Montserrat Caballe, Regine Crespin, Nicolai Gedda, Evelyn Lear, Mildred Miller, Anna Moffo, Birgit Nilsson, Jan Peerce, Roberta Peters, Elisabeth Schwarzkopf, Renata Scotto, Cesare Siepi, Giulietta Simionato, Thoms Stewart, Cesare Valetti and William Warfield. Mr. Wustman has become known to millions of television viewers as the accompanist to Luciano Pavarotti in his many appearances in that medium.

Choice selections for the Vocalist, drawn from the very best solo literature for the voice. Professional artists perform these pieces to guide the singer in interpreting each piece.

___	MMO CD	4041	Beginning Soprano Solos - Kate Hurney
___	MMO CD	4042	Intermediate Soprano Solos - Kate Hurney
___	MMO CD	4043	Beginning Mezzo Soprano Solos - Fay Kittelson
___	MMO CD	4044	Intermediate Mezzo Soprano Solos - Fay Kittelson
___	MMO CD	4045	Advanced Mezzo Soprano Solos - Fay Kittelson
___	MMO CD	4046	Beginning Contralto Solos - Carline Ray
___	MMO CD	4047	Beginning Tenor Solos - George Shirley
___	MMO CD	4048	Intermediate Tenor Solos - George Shirley
___	MMO CD	4049	Advanced Tenor Solos - George Shirley

Music Minus One GUITAR Compact Discs

___	MMO CD	3601	Boccherini: Guitar Quintet, No.4 in D major
___	MMO CD	3602	Giuliani: Guitar Quintet in A Major
___	MMO CD	3603	Classic Guitar Duets Easy-Medium
___	MMO CD	3604	Renaissance & Baroque for Two Guitars
___	MMO CD	3605	Classical & Romantic Guitar Duets
___	MMO CD	3606	Guitar and Flute Duets Vol. 1
___	MMO CD	3607	Guitar and Flute Duets Vol. 2
___	MMO CD	3608	Bluegrass Guitar
___	MMO CD	3609	George Barne's Guitar Method
___	MMO CD	3610	How To Play Folk Guitar
___	MMO CD	3611	Favorite Folk Songs For Guitar
___	MMO CD	3612	Jimmy Raney/Jack Wilkins Jam Guitar Sounds
___	MMO CD	3613	Barnes & Kress Guitar Duets

Music Minus One BANJO Compact Discs

___	MMO CD	4401	Bluegrass Banjo
___	MMO CD	4402	Play The Five String Banjo Vol. 1
___	MMO CD	4403	Five String Banjo Method Vol. 2

Music Minus One TENOR SAX Compact Discs

___	MMO CD	4201	Easy Tenor/Sopr. Solos, Student Series, Beg. Level
___	MMO CD	4202	Easy Tenor/Sopr. Solos, Student Series, Vol.2
___	MMO CD	4203	Easy Jazz Duets For Tenor Sax
___	MMO CD	4204	For Saxes Only - Arranged by Bob Wilber

Music Minus One ALTO SAX Compact Discs

___	MMO CD	4101	Easy Alto Sax Solos, Student Series, Beg. Level
___	MMO CD	4102	Easy Alto Sax Solos, Student Series, Vol.2
___	MMO CD	4103	Easy Jazz Duets For Alto Sax
___	MMO CD	4104	For Saxes Only - Arranged by Bob Wilber

Choice selections for the Alto Sax, drawn from the very best solo literature for the instrument. The pieces are performed by the foremost virtuosi of our time, artists affiliated with the New York Philharmonic, Boston, Chicago, Cleveland and Philadelphia Orchestras. The Julliard School, Curtis Institute of Music, Indiana University, University of Toronto and Metropolitan Opera Orchestra.

___	MMO CD	4111	Paul Bordie, Canadian Soloist, Beginning
___	MMO CD	4112	Vincent Abato, Metropolitan Orch. - Beginning
___	MMO CD	4113	Paul Brodie, Canadian Soloist - Intermediate
___	MMO CD	4114	Vincent Abato, Metropolitan Opera - Intermediate
___	MMO CD	4115	Paul Brodie, Canadian Soloist - Advanced
___	MMO CD	4116	Vincent Abato, Metropolitan Opera - Advanced
___	MMO CD	4117	Paul Brodie, Canadian Soloist - Advanced
___	MMO CD	4118	Vincent Abato, Metropolitan Opera - Advanced

Music Minus One DOUBLE BASS Compact Discs

___	MMO CD	4301	David Walter, Julliard School, Beg-Intermediate
___	MMO CD	4302	David Walter, Julliard School, Intermediate-Adv.
___	MMO CD	4303	For Bassists Only
___	MMO CD	4304	The Beat Goes On - Jazz-Funk, Latin, Pop-Rock

Music Minus One DRUMS Compact Discs

___	MMO CD	5001	Modern Jazz Drumming (2 CD Set)
___	MMO CD	5002	For Drummers Only!
___	MMO CD	5003	Wipe Out
___	MMO CD	5004	Sit-in with Jim Chapin
___	MMO CD	5005	Drum Star
___	MMO CD	5006	Drumpadstickskin
___	MMO CD	5009	Classical Percussion, 2 CD set
___	MMO CD	5010	Eight Men in Search of a Drummer

___	MMO CD	3121	18th Century Violin Music with Orchestra
___	MMO CD	3122	Violin Favorites with Orchestra (easy)
___	MMO CD	3123	Violin Favorites with Orchestra (mod. difficult)
___	MMO CD	3124	Violin Favorites with Orchestra (mod. difficult)
___	MMO CD	3125	The Three B's: Bach, Beethoven and Brahms
___	MMO CD	3126	Vivaldi/Vivaldi/Vivaldi
___	MMO CD	3127	Vivaldi - The Four Seasons (2 CD set)
___	MMO CD	3128	Vivaldi Conc. Eb major, Albinoni Conc. A major
___	MMO CD	3129	Vivaldi Concerto in E & C Major
___	MMO CD	3130	Schubert Sonatinas
___	MMO CD	3131	Haydn String Quartet No. 1 in G major
___	MMO CD	3132	Haydn String Quartet No. 2 in D minor
___	MMO CD	3133	Haydn String Quartet No. 3 in C major
___	MMO CD	3134	Haydn String Quartet No. 4 in Bb major
___	MMO CD	3135	Haydn String Quartet No. 5 in D major
___	MMO CD	3136	Haydn String Quartet No. 6 in Eb major

Music Minus One CLARINET Compact Discs

___	MMO CD	3201	Mozart Clarinet Concerto in A Major
___	MMO CD	3202	Weber/Stamitz Clarinet Concerti
___	MMO CD	3203	Spohr Concerto No.1 in C minor
___	MMO CD	3204	Weber Concertino/Beethoven Trio
___	MMO CD	3205	First Chair Clarinet Solos Orchestral Excerpts
___	MMO CD	3206	The Art of the Solo Clarinet Orchestral Excerpts
___	MMO CD	3207	Mozart Clarinet Quintet in A major
___	MMO CD	3208	Brahms Sonatas Opus 120, # 1 & #2
___	MMO CD	3209	Weber: Grand Duo Concertant - Wagner: Adagio
___	MMO CD	3210	Schumann Fantasy Pieces, Three Romances
___	MMO CD	3211	Easy Clarinet Solos, Student Series, 1-3 years
___	MMO CD	3212	Easy Clarinet Solos, Vol. 2
___	MMO CD	3213	Easy Jazz Duets

Choice selections for the Clarinet, drawn from the very best solo literature for the instrument. The pieces are performed by the foremost virtuosi of our time, artists affiliated with the New York Philharmonic, Boston, Chicago, Cleveland and Philadelphia Orchestras. The Julliard School, Curtis Institute of Music, Indiana University, University of Toronto and Metropolitan Opera Ochestra.

___	MMO CD	3221	Jerome Bunke, Clinician - Beginning Level
___	MMO CD	3222	Beginning Contest Solos - Harold Wright
___	MMO CD	3223	Intermediate Contest Solos - Stanley Drucker
___	MMO CD	3224	Intermediate Contest Solos - Julius Baker
___	MMO CD	3225	Advanced Contest Solos - Stanley Drucker
___	MMO CD	3226	Advanced Contest Solos - Harold Wright
___	MMO CD	3227	Intermediate Contest Solos - Stanley Drucker
___	MMO CD	3228	Advanced Contest Solos - Stanley Drucker
___	MMO CD	3229	Advanced Contest Solos - Harold Wright

Music Minus One FLUTE Compact Discs

___	MMO CD	3300	Mozart Concerto in D, Quantz Concerto in G
___	MMO CD	3301	Mozart Concerto in G
___	MMO CD	3302	J.S. Bach Suite #2 in Bm
___	MMO CD	3303	Boccherini in D, Vivaldi #2 in Gm, Mozart Andante
___	MMO CD	3304	Haydn, Vivaldi, Frederick "The Great" Concertos
___	MMO CD	3305	Vivaldi in F, Telemann in D, LeClair in C Concertos
___	MMO CD	3306	Bach Brandenburg Concerto #2, Haydn Conc. in D
___	MMO CD	3307	Bach 'Triple' Concerto in Am, Vivaldi #9 in Dm
___	MMO CD	3308	Mozart Quartet in F, Stamitz Quartet in F
___	MMO CD	3309	Haydn London Trios
___	MMO CD	3310	Bach Brandenburg Concerti #4 & #5
___	MMO CD	3311	Mozart Three Flute Quartets, C - D - A major
___	MMO CD	3313	Flute Song
___	MMO CD	3314	Vivaldi Concerto in D major, G major, F major
___	MMO CD	3315	Vivaldi Concerto in Am, G, D
___	MMO CD	3316	Easy Flute Solos, Student Series, Beginning Level
___	MMO CD	3317	Easy Flute Solos, Student Series, Vol.2
___	MMO CD	3318	Easy Jazz Duets
___	MMO CD	3319	Flute and Guitar Duets Vol. 1
___	MMO CD	3320	Flute and Guitar Duets Vol. 2
___	MMO CD	3333	First Chair Solos

Choice sections for the Flute, drawn from the very best solo literature for the instrument. The pieces are performed by the foremost virtuosi of our time, artists affiliated with the New York Philharmonic, Boston, Chicago, Cleveland and Philadelphia Orchestras. The Julliard School, Curtis Institute of Music, Indiana University, University of Toronto and Metropolitan Opera Orchestra.

___	MMO CD	3321	Murray Panitz, Philadelphia Orch - Beginning
___	MMO CD	3322	Beginning Contest Solos - Donald Peck
___	MMO CD	3323	Julius Baker, NY Philharmonic - Intermediate
___	MMO CD	3324	Intermediate Contest Solos - Donald Peck

___	MMO CD	3325	Murray Panitz, Philadelphia Orch - Advanced
___	MMO CD	3326	Advanced Contest Solos - Julius Baker
___	MMO CD	3327	Intermediate Contest Solos - Donald Peck
___	MMO CD	3328	Murray Panitz, Philadelphia Orch - Beginning
___	MMO CD	3329	Julius Baker, NY Philharmonic - Intermediate
___	MMO CD	3330	Doriot Anthony Dwyer, Boston Symphony- Beginning
___	MMO CD	3331	Doriot Anthony Dwyer, Boston Symphony - Intermed.
___	MMO CD	3332	Doriot Anthony Dwyer, Boston Symphony - Advanced

Music Minus One OBOE Compact Discs

___	MMO CD	3400	Albinoni Concerto Bb, D, & Dm
___	MMO CD	3401	Telemann F minor, Handel #8 Bb major, Vivaldi #9
___	MMO CD	3402	Mozart Quartet F major, Stamitz Quartet F major

Music Minus One FRENCH HORN Compact Discs

___	MMO CD	3501	Mozart Concert i No.2 & No.3
___	MMO CD	3502	Baroque Brass and Beyond, Brass Quintet
___	MMO CD	3503	Music For Brass Quintet

Choice selections for the French Horn, drawn from the very best solo literature for the instrument. The pieces are performed by the foremost virtuosi of our time, artists affiliated with the New York Philharmonic, Boston, Chicago, Cleveland and Philadelphia Orchestras. The Julliard School, Curtis Institute of Music, Indiana University, University of Toronto and Metropolitan opera Orchestra.

___	MMO CD	3511	Beginning Contest Solos
___	MMO CD	3512	Beginning Contest Solos
___	MMO CD	3513	Dale Clevenger, Chicago Symphony - Intermediate
___	MMO CD	3514	Mason Jones, Philadelphia Orchestra - Intermediate
___	MMO CD	3515	Myron Bloom, Cleveland Symphony - Advanced
___	MMO CD	3516	Dale Clevenger, Chicago Symphony - Advanced
___	MMO CD	3517	Mason Jones, Philadelphia Orchestra - Intermediate
___	MMO CD	3518	Myron Bloom, Cleveland Symphony - Advanced
___	MMO CD	3519	Dale Clevenger, Chicago Symphony - Intermediate

Music Minus One CELLO Compact Discs

___	MMO CD	3701	DVORAK Concerto in B Minor
___	MMO CD	3702	C.P.E. Bach Concerto in A minor
___	MMO CD	3703	Boccherini Conc. in Bb, Bruch Kol Nidrei
___	MMO CD	3704	Schumann Concerti Plus Three More
___	MMO CD	3705	Ten Pieces For Cello and Piano
___	MMO CD	3706	Claude Bolling Suite for Cello and Jazz Piano Trio

Music Minus One TRUMPET Compact Discs

___	MMO CD	3801	Three Trumpet Concerti
___	MMO CD	3802	Easy Trumpet Solos, Student Series, Beg. Level
___	MMO CD	3803	Easy Trumpet Solos, Student Series, Vol.2
___	MMO CD	3804	Easy Jazz Duets For Trumpets
___	MMO CD	3805	Music For Brass Ensemble
___	MMO CD	3806	First Chair Trumpet Solos Orchestral Excerpts
___	MMO CD	3807	The Art Of Solo Trumpet
___	MMO CD	3808	Baroque, Brass, And Beyond
___	MMO CD	3809	The Arban Trumpet Duets
___	MMO CD	3810	Sousa Marches and Beethoven/Strauss/Berlioz

Choice selections for the Trumpet, drawn from the very best solo literature for the instrument. The pieces are performed by the foremost virtuosi of our time, artists affiliated with the New York Philharmonic, Boston, Chicago, Cleveland and Philadelphia Orchestras. The Julliard School, Curtis Institute of Music, Indiana University, University of Toronto and Metropolitan Opera Orchestra.

___	MMO CD	3811	Beginning Contest Solos
___	MMO CD	3812	Beginning Contest Solos
___	MMO CD	3813	Intermediate Contest Solos
___	MMO CD	3814	Intermediate Contest Solos
___	MMO CD	3815	Advanced Contest Solos
___	MMO CD	3816	Advanced Contest Solos
___	MMO CD	3817	Intermediate Contest Solos
___	MMO CD	3818	Advanced Contest Solos
___	MMO CD	3819	Advanced Contest Solos
___	MMO CD	3821	Beginning Contest Solos
___	MMO CD	3822	Intermediate Contest Solos

Music Minus One CONTEMPORARY POPULAR Songs

- ____ MMO CDG 101 The Hits of Patsy Cline
- ____ MMO CDG 102 Country Female Hits
- ____ MMO CDG 103 Country Male Hits
- ____ MMO CDG 104 Country Male Classics
- ____ MMO CDG 105 Great Standards
- ____ MMO CDG 107 Pop Female Hits
- ____ MMO CDG 108 Great Love Songs
- ____ MMO CDG 109 Hits of the 60's
- ____ MMO CDG 110 Hits of the 50's
- ____ MMO CDG 111 Children's Favorites
- ____ MMO CDG 112 Christmas Favorites
- ____ MMO CDG 113 Hits of Neil Diamond Vol. 1
- ____ MMO CDG 114 The Carpenters
- ____ MMO CDG 115 Hits of Elton John
- ____ MMO CDG 116 Hits of Barbara Streisand
- ____ MMO CDG 117 Hits of Frank Sinatra
- ____ MMO CDG 118 Hits of Elvis Presley
- ____ MMO CDG 119 World's Greatest Sing-Alongs
- ____ MMO CDG 120 Hits of Bette Midler
- ____ MMO CDG 121 Best of Broadway
- ____ MMO CDG 122 Hits of Whitney Houston
- ____ MMO CDG 123 Hits of Linda Ronstadt
- ____ MMO CDG 124 Old Tyme Sing-Alongs
- ____ MMO CDG 125 Hits of Neil Diamond Vol. 2
- ____ MMO CDG 126 Happy Songs Are Here Again
- ____ MMO CDG 127 The Coasters & The Drifters
- ____ MMO CDG 128 Love Songs For A Wedding
- ____ MMO CDG 129 The Platters
- ____ MMO CDG 130 Male Chart Toppers
- ____ MMO CDG 131 Pop Male Hits
- ____ MMO CDG 132 Female Chart Toppers
- ____ MMO CDG 133 Pop Female Hits
- ____ MMO CDG 134 Country Males
- ____ MMO CDG 135 Country Females
- ____ MMO CDG 137 Hits of Neil Diamond Vol. 3
- ____ MMO CDG 1001 Hits of Frank Sinatra
- ____ MMO CDG 1002 Hits of Barbara Streisand
- ____ MMO CDG 1004 Hits of Elvis Presley
- ____ MMO CDG 1005 Hits of the Beatles
- ____ MMO CDG 1008 Hits of Roy Orbison
- ____ MMO CDG 1009 Hits of Patsy Cline
- ____ MMO CDG 1011 Hits of Billy Joel
- ____ MMO CDG 1012 Hits of Linda Ronstadt
- ____ MMO CDG 1013 Hits of the Carpenters
- ____ MMO CDG 1017 Hits of Ray Charles
- ____ MMO CDG1019 Hits of Anita Baker
- ____ MMO CDG1020 Hits of Sammy Davis Jr./Anthony Newley
- ____ MMO CDG1024 George Gershwin Favorites
- ____ MMO CDG1025 Songs of Cole Porter
- ____ MMO CDG1027 Hits of Diana Ross
- ____ MMO CDG1028 Hits of Tom Jones
- ____ MMO CDG1029 Hits of Bobby Darin & Frank Sinatra
- ____ MMO CDG1032 Hits of Nat "King" Cole
- ____ MMO CDG1036 Female Groups of the 60s
- ____ MMO CDG1038 Male Groups of the 60s
- ____ MMO CDG1039 The Beach Boys
- ____ MMO CDG1043 Hits of Kenny Rogers
- ____ MMO CDG1045 Hits of Luther Vandross
- ____ MMO CDG1049 Hits of Elvis Presley
- ____ MMO CDG1052 Hits of Bonnie Rait
- ____ MMO CDG1055 Hits of Harrty Connick Jr.
- ____ MMO CDG1060 Hits of Tina Turner
- ____ MMO CDG1064 Hits of Rod Stewart
- ____ MMO CDG1065 Hits of Englebert Humperdinck
- ____ MMO CDG1066 Hits of Rock and Roll
- ____ MMO CDG1071 Karaoke Party
- ____ MMO CDG1072 James Taylor
- ____ MMO CDG1074 Elvis at the Movies
- ____ MMO CDG1083 Songs For A Wedding Vol. 1
- ____ MMO CDG1084 Sings For A Wedding Vol. 2
- ____ MMO CDG1085 Hits of Michael Bolton
- ____ MMO CDG1087 Female Hits of the 90's
- ____ MMO CDG1088 Karaoke D.J. Party
- ____ MMO CDG1089 Country Karaoke for Women
- ____ MMO CDG1090 Country Karaoke for Men
- ____ MMO CDG1200 Hits of Bette Midler
- ____ MMO CDG1201 Hootie and the Blowfish
- ____ MMO CDG1202 Hits of Regina Belle
- ____ MMO CDG1203 Christmas Memories

Music Minus One BROADWAY Shows

- ____ MMO CD 1016 Les Miserables/Phantom of the Opera
- ____ MMO CD 1054 Hits of Andrew Llyod Webber
- ____ MMO CD 1067 Guys And Dolls
- ____ MMO CD 1100 West Side Story (2 CD set)
- ____ MMO CD 1110 Cabaret (2 CD Set)
- ____ MMO CD 1173 Camelot
- ____ MMO CD 1130 Best of Andrew Lloyd Webber
- ____ MMO CD 1133 The Sound of Broadway
- ____ MMO CD 1134 Broadway Melodies
- ____ MMO CD 1144 Barbra's Broadway
- ____ MMO CD 1151 Jekyll & Hyde
- ____ MMO CD 1174 My Fair Lady (2 CD Set)
- ____ MMO CD 1175 Oklahoma!
- ____ MMO CD 1176 The Sound of Music
- ____ MMO CD 1177 South Pacific
- ____ MMO CD 1178 The King And I
- ____ MMO CD 1179 Fiddler On The Roof (2 CD set)
- ____ MMO CD 1180 Carousel
- ____ MMO CD 1181 Porgy and Bess
- ____ MMO CD 1183 The Music Man
- ____ MMO CD 1184 Showboat
- ____ MMO CD 1187 Hello Dolly! (2 CD Set)
- ____ MMO CD 1189 Oliver (2 CD Set)
- ____ MMO CD 1193 Sunset Boulevard
- ____ MMO CD 1196 Grease
- ____ MMO CD 1197 Smokey Joe's Cafe

Music Minus One PIANO Compact Discs

- ____ MMO CD 3001 Beethoven Concerto #1 in C
- ____ MMO CD 3002 Beethoven Concerto #2 in Bb
- ____ MMO CD 3003 Beethoven Concerto #3 in Cm
- ____ MMO CD 3004 Beethoven Concerto #4 in G major
- ____ MMO CD 3005 Beethoven Concerto #5 in Eb major (2 CD set)
- ____ MMO CD 3006 Grieg Concerto
- ____ MMO CD 3007 Rachmaninoff Concerto #2
- ____ MMO CD 3008 Schumann Concerto in A minor, Op. 54
- ____ MMO CD 3009 Brahms Concerto #1 in D minor (2 CD set)
- ____ MMO CD 3010 Chopin Concerto #1
- ____ MMO CD 3011 Mendelssohn Concerto #1 in G minor
- ____ MMO CD 3012 Mozart Concerto #9
- ____ MMO CD 3013 Mozart Concerto #12
- ____ MMO CD 3014 Mozart Concerto #20
- ____ MMO CD 3015 Mozart Concerto #23
- ____ MMO CD 3016 Mozart Concerto #24
- ____ MMO CD 3017 Mozart Piano Concerto No.26 in D "Coronation"
- ____ MMO CD 3018 Mozart Concerto in G major
- ____ MMO CD 3019 Liszt Concerto #1/Weber Concertstuk, Op. 79
- ____ MMO CD 3020 Liszt Concerto #2 - Hungarian Fantasia
- ____ MMO CD 3021 Bach Concerto in F minor, J.C. Bach in Eb
- ____ MMO CD 3022 Bach Concerto in Dm
- ____ MMO CD 3023 Haydn Concerto in D
- ____ MMO CD 3024 The Heart Of The Piano Concerto
- ____ MMO CD 3025 Themes From The Great Piano Concerti
- ____ MMO CD 3026 Tschaikovsky Concerto #1
- ____ MMO CD 3033 The Art of Popular Piano Playing Vol. 1
- ____ MMO CD 3034 The Art of Popular Piano Playing Vol. 2
- ____ MMO CD 3035 Pop Piano For Starters

Music Minus One VIOLIN Compact Discs VIOLIN

- ____ MMO CD 3100 Bruch Concerto
- ____ MMO CD 3101 Mendelssohn Concerto
- ____ MMO CD 3102 Tschaikovsky Concerto
- ____ MMO CD 3103 J.S. Bach "Double" Concerto
- ____ MMO CD 3104 J.S. Bach Concerto in E & Am
- ____ MMO CD 3105 J.S. Bach Brandenburg Concerti #4 & #5
- ____ MMO CD 3106 J.S. Bach Brandenburg #2, Triple Concerto
- ____ MMO CD 3107 J.S. Bach Concerto in Dm
- ____ MMO CD 3108 BRAHMS Concerto in D
- ____ MMO CD 3109 Chausson Poeme, Schubert Rondo
- ____ MMO CD 3110 Lalo Symphonic Espagnole
- ____ MMO CD 3111 Mozart Concerto in D, Vivaldi Concerto in Am
- ____ MMO CD 3112 Mozart Concerto in A
- ____ MMO CD 3114 Viotti Concerto #22
- ____ MMO CD 3115 Beethoven Two Romances/"Spring" Sonata
- ____ MMO CD 3116 St.-Saens Intro/Rondo Capriccioso, Mozart Serenade
- ____ MMO CD 3117 Beethoven Concerto in D major (2 CD set)
- ____ MMO CD 3118 The Concertmaster (Symphonic Excerpts)
- ____ MMO CD 3119 Air on a G String (Favorite Encores)
- ____ MMO CD 3120 Concert Pieces for the Serious Violinist

MMO MUSIC GROUP, INC., 50 Executive Boulevard, Elmsford, NY 10523-1325